The Taj Mahal: The History of India's Most Famous Monument
By Jesse Harasta and Charles River Editors

Picture by Muhammad Mahdi Karim

About Charles River Editors

Charles River Editors provides superior editing and original writing services across the digital publishing industry, with the expertise to create digital content for publishers across a vast range of subject matter. In addition to providing original digital content for third party publishers, we also republish civilization's greatest literary works, bringing them to new generations of readers via ebooks.

Introduction

Picture by Bjørn Christian Tørrissen

The Taj Mahal

"Should guilty seek asylum here,
Like one pardoned, he becomes free from sin.
Should a sinner make his way to this mansion,
All his past sins are to be washed away.
The sight of this mansion creates sorrowing sighs;
And the sun and the moon shed tears from their eyes.
In this world this edifice has been made;
To display thereby the creator's glory." – Emperor Shah Jahan's description of the Taj Mahal

Taj Mahal is Arabic for "crown of palaces", and the name could not be more fitting for one of the most instantly recognizable buildings in the world. Constructed over a span of about 20 years in the mid-17th century as a mausoleum for the wife of Emperor Shah Jahan, the Taj Mahal is aptly described by UNESCO, which designated it a World Heritage site, as "the jewel of Muslim art in India and one of the universally admired masterpieces of the world's heritage". Indeed, the Taj Mahal is truly a global icon because it masterfully fused the artistic and architectural elements of several cultures, including Indian, Ottoman, Persian, and Islamic cultures across the region.

While the marble dome is the first feature that pops out about the Taj Mahal, the careful layout of the entire structure is also incredibly impressive, and it took thousands of laborers several years to work on the other features, from the gardens to the calligraphy inscribed on the exterior. The Taj Mahal also includes other buildings, including a mosque and other tombs and mausoleums for people close to the emperor.

Not surprisingly, given the scope and quality of the work, the Taj Mahal has fascinated people around the world for centuries, and naturally, all sorts of myths about it have sprung up. For the most part, however, people are simply drawn to it today as one of the premiere tourist sites in the world, and millions of people come from around the world to visit it every year.

The Taj Mahal: The History of India's Most Famous Monument chronicles the origins, construction, and history of the Taj Mahal over the last 350 years. Along with pictures of important people, places, and events, you will learn about one of the world's most famous memorials like you never have before.

Chapter 1: A Great Love Story?

"The Taj Mahal rises above the banks of the river like a solitary tear suspended on the cheek of time." - Rabindranath Tagore, Bengali Nobel Laureate Poet

"Rahul had wondered how someone could love their beloved so much that their dedication to them became one of the wonders of the world." - Faraaz Kazi, modern novelist

"Marble, I perceive, covers a multitude of sins." - Aldous Huxley, author of *Brave New World*

At its heart, the Taj Mahal - the greatest triumph of Persian and Mughal architecture, a widely recognized modern wonder of the world, and the prize of India - is a story about love and devotion. Its designer, the Mughal Emperor Shah Jahan, created it as the tomb and memorial to his beloved wife Mumtaz Mahal. The soaring marble dome, towers reaching to the heavens, and lush formal gardens all sing out testimony to his love for her. Or so the story goes.

The Taj Mahal's purpose as a mausoleum, and an incredible one at that, has long led many to credit its origins to the fairy-tale love of Shah Jahan and Mumtaz Mahal, a guiding myth told for the millions of visitors annually. As Rabindranath Tagore described so beautifully, in this tale it is a "solitary tear suspended on the cheek of time," an attempt to commemorate a feeling for a person in the grandest manner possible. Perhaps not surprisingly, parts of this overarching story have a basis in fact, but much of it includes later innovation, fabrication, and imagination.

Illustration depicting Emperor Shah Jahan

The agreed-upon facts are straightforward. Shah Jahan (1592-1666) was the fifth emperor of the Mughal Empire, a mighty Muslim-ruled state that dominated most of today's northern India, Pakistan and Afghanistan until they were eclipsed and eventually destroyed by the British in the 18th century. Jahan was an ambitious man of royal lineage who came to the throne in 1628 through a combination of military conquest and adroit politicking, and during his reign he expanded the empire and accomplished a number of feats of city planning and monumental architecture (of which the Taj is only the most famous example). He ruled until he was deposed and imprisoned by his son Aurangzeb in 1658.

The Shah, a title last used by the Shahs of Iran, had six wives, even though up to four are normally permitted by Islamic law, but accounts agree that his relationship with his third wife, Mumtaz Mahal, was unusually close. Mumtaz, whose name means "chosen one of the palace" in Persian, was by all accounts a beautiful noble woman, and the two of them were so inseparable that she accompanied him on his journeys. In kind, she also wielded considerable power behind the throne after elbowing out a rival wife, Arjumand Banu Begum, and in the end, she was the custodian of the royal seal, which meant that laws could not be made official without her review. Unfortunately, in 1630, shortly after her husband's ascendancy to the throne, she died at age 40 due to complications of childbirth. In total, she gave birth to seven children, including the sixth emperor, Aurangzeb[1].

A posthumous Mughal painting that depicts Mumtaz Mahal.

Accounts of the time note that the Shah and his family were crushed by the news. The oldest daughter, Princess Jahanara is said to have given away her jewels in her grief, and the Emperor himself retreated from romantic overtures with his other wives and never bore another child.

---

1 "Taj Mahal" at the *Encyclopedia Britannica Online* accessed online at: http://www.britannica.com/EBchecked/topic/581007/Taj-Mahal

Most importantly, he took an unprecedented step amongst the members of his dynasty and decided to construct an elaborate mausoleum for his deceased wife, the end product of which was the Taj Mahal - the "Crown of the Palaces."[2]

These events are widely agreed-upon by historians, but a lot has been added onto this set of facts over the centuries. In the European imagination, this is due in large measure to the fact that European commentators largely began encountering the Taj during the Romantic period, when they were already pre-disposed to celebrate incredible displays of emotional feeling and the concept of romantic love, itself a relatively new development in European thinking. Since that time, the tales about the Taj have gradually grown in the telling. For example, after being deposed, the Shah was imprisoned for the rest of his life in the Agra Fort only a few miles from the Taj, and tour guides tell how the Shah must have ended his days looking out his window at the outline of the tomb in the distance. While that is certainly romantic and altogether possible, there are no records documenting that. Moreover, the idea that the Shah planned to have his own tomb, a mirror of the Taj but in black marble, built facing across the river is also an idea of recent invention.

---

2   "Taj Mahal Story" accessed online at: http://famouswonders.com/taj-mahal-story/

The view of the Taj Mahal from the Agra Fort. Picture by Kanithapithan

These inventions aside, is the story really true? Did the Shah love his wife so deeply? While the idea that the Taj is an "elegy in marble" and a "tear ... on the cheek of time" is certainly the dominant narrative about the Taj - possibly because it continues to entrance millions - it has never been the only one. Perhaps the most critical author of the site to write in English was Aldous Huxley, who argued that the building, while grand in scale, was built of inferior materials and in a weak, derivative style. Huxley also believed that the Taj Mahal was at most a grand propaganda piece for an emperor who should be better known for his ruthlessness than for his romance[3]. Advocates of that approach note that in the early 1630s, Jahan had just consolidated his control over a spectacular and growing empire, and that the new ruler probably wanted to construct some type of monument that would be a symbol of his power, the way the ancient Egyptian pharaohs frequently tried to outdo their predecessors with new pyramids. If so, something on the scale of the Taj Mahal may have come about even without the death of one of his several wives.

Which argument has more weight? In truth, the evidence from records of the period is mixed. The Shah's court was Persian in character, and Persian writings of the day (like the writings of the Romantic 18th century English) were known to be florid in their descriptions and overflowing with tales of sorrow and emotion. In other words, the story of Jahan's love seems to fit within that genre, making it possible that the Persian scribes added a sense of grandeur that may not have actually existed. Moreover, most accounts of the day, including official British diplomatic reports, describe Jahan as arrogant and supremely self-centered. They also reported his continued attentions to both his wives and to other lovers, including reports of incestuous affairs with Princess Jahanara being brought to the attention of Muslim authorities. While these reports are broadly ignored in the tale of the Taj, they bring an extra layer of complexity to the actual history[4].

The Taj Mahal as a monument might also offer some clues. The construction of a grand mausoleum for a wife had no precedent in any of the architectural traditions that the Mughals blended (including Muslim, Persian, Hindu and Mongol influences), and such a project was not repeated afterwards. Moreover, there is no similar commemoration of a wife in any other culture of the world; the only mausoleums of similar grandeur are all dedicated to male rulers (such as the Great Pyramid of Giza dedicated to Khufu or the Kumsusan Palace of the Sun in North Korea that houses Kim Il-Sung and Kim Jong-Il). It seems to evoke the mournful love like similar elegies for deceased wives like Niel Gow's "Lament for the Death of his Second Wife."

Even if Shah Jahan would have constructed some sort of monument in the first years of his

---

3 "Aldous Huxley on the Taj Mahal" by Aldous Huxley in the journal *MARG*. V 4, no 2, p 15-20
4 "The Myth of the Taj Mahal and a New Theory of its Symbolic Meaning" by Wayne E. Begley in the journal *Art Bulletin* V 61, No 1, pp 7-37

reign without the death of a wife, the fact that he may have chosen to commemorate his companion in such a way is revealing not of the character of the man so much as the strength of his feeling. If the widely believed story about the origins of the Taj Mahal is true, perhaps the greatest lesson it teaches viewers is that one didn't need to be a saint to love deeply or completely pure of heart to mourn completely.

Chapter 2: The Mughal Empire

The motivation for creating the Taj may still be an open question, but ultimately, it was the Mughal Empire and its Persian influences that made the Taj Mahal possible by creating a cultural context that made the monument a synthesis of Muslim, Persian, and Hindu architecture.

The Mughals were one of the great dynastic empires of the early Modern period, competing with the Shahs of Persia and the Ottomans of Istanbul for the title of the greatest Muslim-ruled state of its time. Like the dynasties of both of these other empires, the Mughals were descendants of nomadic Central Asian tribes that traced their ancestry to both the Mongol Khans (where their name "Mughal" originates) and the Turkic tribes. For example, the first Mughal Emperor Babur (r. 1526-1530) claimed a lineage on his mother's side from Genghis Khan's second son Chagatai and the great Turkic leader Timur on his father's side. Driven from the steppes, Babur established a base in the city of Kabul (today the capital of Afghanistan), and from there he conquered south and east over much of today's Pakistan and northern India, including the populous areas of Punjab and then over the Sultan of Delhi[5]. Throughout the two centuries and seven emperors of the Mughal dynasty, the realm was known for its able administrators, distinctive architecture, and its relative religious harmony.

After Babur, perhaps the best known emperor was Akbar the Great, who ruled from 1556-1605, a reign of considerable length. Under the rule of Akbar, the Mughal court was known for its religious tolerance, and the non-Muslim majorities of his realm (primarily Hindus) were fully integrated into the intellectual and political life of the empire. In fact, Akbar promoted a new religion of his own creation called Din-e-Illahi, which fused Islam and Hinduism with elements of Christianity and Zoroastrianism. While Din-e-Illahi may have been a personality cult around the Emperor that never had widespread acceptance and all but died with him, it did reveal the Mughal emperor's willingness to adapt his Islamic background to an Indian context.[6]

In addition to its adoption of indigenous cultural traits, the Mughal court also borrowed heavily from neighboring Persia, even though the Persians were rivals of the Mughals. In fact, they battled over the territory of today's Afghanistan, and the great Persian emperor Nader Shah eventually sacked Delhi and stole Shah Jahan's dazzling Peacock Throne in 1639. Nevertheless,

---

5 "Mughal Dynasty" at the *Encyclopedia Britannica Online*. Accessed online at: http://www.britannica.com/EBchecked/topic/396125/Mughal-dynasty
6 "Din-i-Ilahi" at the *Encyclopedia Britannica Online* . Accessed online at: http://www.britannica.com/EBchecked/topic/163768/Din-i-Ilahi

the Persians were the dominant cultural power of southern Asia at the time, and courts from Istanbul to Bengal all emulated Persian styles and often adopted Farsi (the Persian language) as administrative tongues[7]. This was similar to the manner in which the French language and the French court's customs dominated medieval Europe all the way to the courts of the Russian Czars, despite the fact that many of those kingdoms were rivals of France.

The Mughals not only adopted Persian culture and customs, including poetry and art, but also brought large numbers of Persians into the Empire as administrators, something a number of Arab Caliphs had done long before. This meant that by the time of Shah Jahan ("Shah" itself being a Farsi term), the Mughal court could no longer be considered Mongol-Turkic but instead fundamentally Persian in character, a cultural extension of the Persian heartland into Northern India[8]. That said, this did not, of course, trickle down into the common folk, who remained largely Hindu and spoke Sanskrit-derived languages.

Together, Persian and Hindu influences combined to help bring about the architectural design of the Taj Mahal, but the Persians may have also influenced the purpose of the Taj's very existence. Tombs have long played a central place in the world of Persian architecture, religion and social status, and even though the Mughal Shahs were Sunni Muslims, they and their empire were deeply influenced by religious currents emerging out of the Shi'a Persia; in fact, Mumtaz Mahal appears to have been a Shiite herself. At its heart, the Sunni-Shi'a divide was about how to choose leaders ("Caliphs"). The Sunnis believed that Caliphs did not have to possess any particular spiritual knowledge, and that instead they were to maintain order and protect Islamic learning and should be chosen by community consensus. The Shi'a, on the other hand, argued that the descendants of the Prophet Mohammed - particularly of his daughter Fatima and his cousin Ali - were blessed by Allah with spiritual insights and the power to govern with proper justice and piety. Because of this, the Shi'a have always venerated the Prophet's descendants and, importantly for the history of the Taj, have built shrines over the places of their burials. This means that, unlike the Sunni, the Shi'a religious landscape is dotted with shrines dedicated to various saintly figures[9].

As the stronghold of the Shi'a since the Safavid Dynasty (1501-1736), Iran/Persia fused this fascination with mausoleums with their own indigenous interest in such buildings. Persians had long built spectacular tombs like the Mausoleum of Cyrus the Great and the royal necropolis at Naqsh-e Rustam (which included the tombs of Darius the Great and Xerxes I amongst others), but the nomadic peoples of Central Asia that the Mughals descended from did not have an

---

7 "Persian Influence in Bangla (Bengali) Literature." Accessed online at: http://write-translate.blogspot.com/2006/02/persian-influence-in-bangla-bengali.html
8 *Role of Persians at the Mughal Court: A Historical Study, during 1526 A.D. to 1707 A.D.* by Muhammad Ziauddin (2005). Unpublished PhD Thesis submitted to the University of Balochistan. Accessed online at: http://www.scribd.com/doc/59873962/23/Persians-in-the-Politics-and-Administration-of-Babur-and-Humayun
9 *The Shia Revival: How Conflicts within Islam Will Shape the Future* by Vali Nasr (2006). W.W. Norton Company: New York.

elaborate tradition of mausoleums. Genghis Khan famously requested an unmarked grave, and the Tibetan Buddhists allowed their remains to be devoured by birds.

However, when the Mughals entered India, they wholeheartedly adopted the Persian burial traditions, and even before the Taj Mahal, there were several Mughal garden tombs. The Emperor Humayun, Babur's son and Akbar's father, built the first one in Delhi, creating the style of garden tombs in 1570. For Humayun, the architects designed the charbagh style of garden and placed his mausoleum in its center, much like the positioning of the Taj Mahal. Furthermore, like the Taj itself, Humayun's mausoleum was topped with an onion dome and flanked by chhartis, and it is also recognized as a UNESCO World Heritage Site[10]. Akbar's Tomb can be found in Agra near the Taj Mahal, and it also possesses a deeply Islamic-influenced façade, including an iwan gate and two minaret-like towers[11].

Humayun's Tomb. Picture by Muhammad Mahdi Karim

Another tomb predecessor was the mausoleum of Jahangir, the father of Shah Jahan himself. Located in Lahore, Pakistan, it is also located within an enclosed charbagh garden, but instead of having a central domed structure, it is a low structure with minaret-like towers at each of the four corners. Jahangir's tomb dates to 1605 and is decorated in a style of mosaics and tiles similar to that of the Taj itself[12], and perhaps not coincidentally, if the designs of Humayun's Tomb and Jahangir's mausoleum were combined and constructed out of white marble, it would form the basic outline of the Taj.

---

10 "Humayun's Tomb, Delhi" on the webpage of the UNESCO World Heritage Site Network. Accessed online at: http://whc.unesco.org/en/list/232
11 "Mausoleum of Akbar" on archnet.org. Accessed online at: http://archnet.org/library/sites/one-site.jsp?site_id=2257
12 "Tombs of Jahangir, Asif Khan and Akbari Sarai, Lahore" on the list of Tentative UNESCO World Heritage Sites. Accessed online at: http://whc.unesco.org/en/tentativelists/1279/

Together, all of these predecessors show how local and foreign influences regarding designs, architecture, and the importance of tombs all combined to help inspire and guide the designers of the Taj. Indeed, the combined Persian-cum-Mughal style of shrine-like mausoleums evolved into the full-blown Mughal charbagh that saw its ultimate expression in the creation of the Taj Mahal. To recognize how these cultural traditions eventually flowed into the masterpiece is not to diminish the genius of the work but to understand how the broader social and cultural histories inevitably influenced art and artists.[13]

Chapter 2: The Architectural History of the Taj Mahal

While the idea of building a mausoleum on a grand scale for one's wife was a new one in the Mughal context, and the eventual building was remarkable for its scale and beauty, the architecture itself was not unprecedented but instead (like all Mughal architecture) a fusion of numerous Asian architectural and aesthetic influences.[14]

The term "Mughal" comes from the same origin as the English term "Mongol", and the Mughals were certainly descendants of the notorious Central Asian nomadic warriors. As the Turkic-speaking Mughals swept into the subcontinent of India in the 16th century, their distant linguistic cousins were founding the Ottoman Empire in today's Turkey. Between these two great empires was the Persian Empire, which at that time was approaching the apex of its power under the Shiite, Turkic-speaking Safavid Dynasty. At this point, the great Muslim cities of Baghdad and Damascus were eclipsed by the cultural splendor of the Safavid city of Isfahan, and the Mughals, under this influence, came to speak not Turkish but Persian as the first language of the court. In the same way, the Safavids themselves were "Persianized" by the people they ruled.[15]

However, in addition to the Persian influence, the Mughals encountered a land that had its own traditions of architecture, art, philosophy, and courtly elegance. The Hindu world had possessed its own great empires, including that of Ashoka the Great, and the Mughals were influenced by their cultural traditions as well. Even today, the cultural remnants of this mingling of traditions continues in the Islam practiced in India, Pakistan and Afghanistan, as well as the Urdu language of Pakistan, which all show deep influences of the Central Asian nomadic invasions, the Arab tradition of the Qur'an, the poetic and artistic practices of Persia and the ancient indigenous practices of South Asia[16].

Muslim Influences

---

13 "Taj Mahal, Agra" on the webpage of the UNESCO World Heritage Site Network. Accessed online at: http://whc.unesco.org/en/list/252
14 "Architecture" at the Taj Mahal Homepage. Accessed online at: http://www.tajmahal.gov.in/architecture2.html
15 "Taj Mahal" at the *National Geographic* World Heritage Guide. Accessed online at: http://travel.nationalgeographic.com/travel/world-heritage/taj-mahal/
16 *Living Islam: Muslim Religious Experience in Pakistan's North-West Frontier* by Magnus Marsden (2005). Cambridge University Press: Cambridge and New York.

At its core, the Taj Mahal is a Muslim building, something so obvious even to casual observers that many inquire whether it is a mosque. The central dome surrounded by spindly towers, and the obvious Muslim influences on the grand front gate, all seem to evoke an iconic image of a grand mosque with its minarets. The towers are of a similar construction to minarets, with three levels of balconies like South Asian minarets.[17] A more careful look shows that the mausoleum is in fact not a mosque, but that the Muslim impression is a good hunch.

The eastern side of the Taj Mahal with the minarets around it

---

17 An image here: http://static.panoramio.com/photos/large/36077790.jpg

Looking upward at a minaret.

The most important external clues that the mausoleum is not a mosque are that its great central gate faces south and the building is oriented on a north-south axis. By Muslim law, all mosques must face towards the holy city of Mecca, which is true of the one mosque actually on the property, a building to the east side of the main mausoleum that is understandably overshadowed by its larger neighbor.

The mosque. Picture by Muhammad Mahdi Karim

Another clue to its Islamic influences is the relative lack of adornment. In the Indian subcontinent, Hindu temples are often festooned with images of gods, demons and other mythological beings, and in some cases, like the famous temples of the southern city of Madurai, the temples' facades appear to be composed entirely of such images[18]. In contrast, the Muslim buildings are decorated with geometric patterns, images of plants and elaborate Arabic calligraphy.

---

18 Images can be found at this gallery:
http://www.flickr.com/photos/lauraelaine/galleries/72157626985824334/#photo_4332285619

Calligraphy on one of the walls of the Taj Mahal

Persian Influences

Mughal architecture can be considered a branch of the broader school of Persian aesthetics, and the grand entryway of the Taj is similar to mosques throughout the Persian world, including the Jama Masjid in Delhi and the stunning structures of the Naqsh-e Jahan Square in Iran's city of Isfahan.

The Naqsh-e Jahan Square. Picture by Arad Mojtahedi

The Naqsh-e Jahan Square is a useful comparison to see the elements that are shared with the Taj Mahal. Like the Taj Mahal, the Square is a complex of buildings rather than a single structure, bounded by a rectilinear design where visitors pass through a central garden area while observing the buildings from a distance. The focus is upon the grand ceremonial gateways and the onion domes of the mosques, though in Isfahan, there is considerably more color in the buildings, unlike the uniform white marble of the Taj[19].

While Mumtaz Mahal was not a holy woman, she was (like most Persians) a Shi'a Muslim, and Shi'as have always had a deep reverence for women in the Qur'an, like Fatima Zahra (the Prophet's only daughter) and Zaynab bint Ali (the Prophet's granddaughter). They also have a tradition of constructing grand shrines over the sites of their tombs. While far simpler in style than the Taj Mahal, the Mosque over the tomb of Zaynab in Damascus (Sayyidah Zaynab Mosque) is one such tomb, and it has a broad paved courtyard with a single grand entrance, a minaret, and an onion dome behind it. Grander still is the tomb to a more distant female relation to the Prophet: Fatema Mæ'sume, the sister of the Eighth Imam. In the Persian holy city of Qom, it has more colorful echoes of the grandeur of the Taj[20]. It would appear that Shah Jahan had the

---

19 For a virtual tour of the Square, visit here: http://stockholm360.net/list.php?id=esfahan
20 *Lady Fatima Masuma (a) of Qum* by Masuma Jaffer. Accessed online at: http://www.al-islam.org/lady-fatima-masuma-of-qum-masuma-jaffer

mausoleums of saintly women like these in mind when he ordered the construction of his wife's final resting place.

Indian and Turkic Influence

Despite the assertions of some far-right Indian nationalists, the Taj Mahal is fundamentally a Persian Muslim building. However, the builders had already begun to draw in Hindu influences, most notably the Indian architectural school of Vastu Shastra, and Shah Jahan's mother was a Hindu from Rajasthan.

Part of this influence is the rectilinear layout: the Taj's central structure has four equal sides, each with a gate and smaller gates at the corners. While the exterior of the building has a prominent central gate overlooking the gardens that is featured in innumerable pictures, the interior is purely symmetrical. In this way it appears to resemble a Hindu Temple, as Vastu Shastra teaches about a balance between four elements through rectilinear structures. In contrast, the contemporary Mughal Mosque of the Jama Masjid in Delhi has an axis directed toward Mecca and is not symmetrical[21]. Likewise, the Taj appears to follow the Vastu Shastra teaching that the height and width of the building should correspond to each other, a harmoniousness that allows the outer towers to stand out visually and add to the striking appearance of the exterior[22]. Other Hindu elements brought into the structure include the use of the four chatris (small domed pavilions standing on pillars) alongside the primary dome.

---

21 Plans of the Jama Masjid can be found here: http://ahmedabad.page.tl/Photos_JAMA-MASJID--s--AHMADABAD.htm
22 "Taj Mahal" in *The Dictionary of Islamic Architecture* at ArchNet. Accessed online at: http://archnet.org/library/dictionary/entry.jsp?entry_id=DIA0864&mode=full

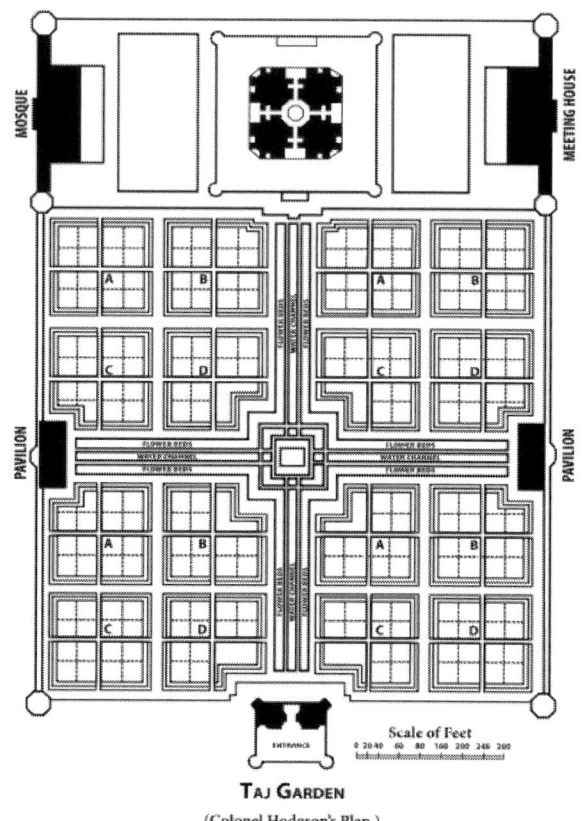

The layout of the Taj Mahal

Facing the Taj Mahal from the great gate. Picture by Shobhit Gosain.

The Turkic influence on the structure is even more subtle, given the relative paucity of architectural tradition amongst the nomadic peoples of Central Asia. In fact, most of the grandest buildings in modern Central Asia are of a Persian-influence style in places like Bukhara and Samarkhand. The Turkic influence is not to be seen in the buildings themselves but rather the fact that the tombs are placed at the hearts of gardens, unlike any in the Persian tradition. The Mughals, perhaps drawing upon Central Asian traditions of burial out-of-doors, developed distinctive tomb-gardens, of which the Taj is the most celebrated example.

The Taj as an Influence

While numerous artistic trends flowed into the imaginations of the Taj's creators, any building of such scale, fame and grandeur must in turn influence later works. One of the greatest effects of the Taj Mahal has been as a poster child for Indian and Mughal architecture to the world; as one of the world's most iconic buildings, there is no modern student of the design or history of buildings that is not familiar with it.

Today, when an architect seeks to emulate an "Indian" style, especially one associated with royal grandeur or Oriental luxury, the tendency is to draw upon the Mughal style and, especially, the Taj Mahal. Indian luxury hotels , especially those seeking an international clientele, often include chhatris, onion domes, crenelated walls and elaborate tiles and mosaics. Even the tackier side of Orientalism, such as the "Corn Palace" of Mitchell, South Dakota, possesses onion domes, chhatri-esque minarets and fierce devotion to perfect symmetry[23].

Building the Taj

Once Shah Jahan had the project in mind, he gave a large palace to a man named Maharajah Jai Singh as a trade for the land on which the Taj Mahal would sit. The project, which required an estimated 20,000 workers, first went about excavating land to deal with its proximity to the Yamuna River, which included steps like filling the foundations with dirt above the banks of the river. At the same time, the project required different kinds of materials, some of which came from India but much of which was only located in other spots across the continent. For example, the white marble came from places like Makrana, while turquoise came from Tibet and crystal came from China, so workers were dispatched with hundreds of elephants to find the necessary materials and carry them back.

For the mausoleum itself, the laborers made a scaffold so extensive that the designers were afraid it would take years to safely remove, so the emperor allegedly let the people know they could take bricks from the scaffolding, thereby speeding up the process. After that, an earthen ramp was constructed on which the building's materials could be moved to the site, and these materials were so heavy that some of it required having 30 oxen to move them. Once the materials had arrived, the laborers used pulleys to raise the marble into place. That entire process took about 12 years to complete, and that didn't include construction of the other parts of the Taj Mahal, including its soaring minarets, the great gate, and the mosque on the site. It would take another decade for the rest to be completed.

Of course, in addition to building the actual Taj Mahal, it had to be decorated, and artisans were brought from across the continent to work on it. For example, calligraphy was done by men hailing from Syria and Persia, while marble sculptors and stonecutters came from other parts of India.

---

23 For more on the fascinating, ever-changing Corn Palace, visit: http://www.cornpalace.org/

Chapter 3: The Ground Plan from South to North

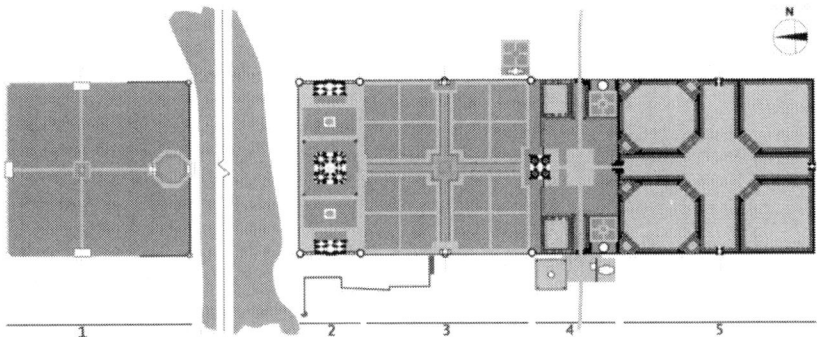

The ground plan of the Taj Mahal facing east:

1. The Moonlight Garden north of the river Yamuna.

2. The riverfront terrace, which includes the Mausoleum, Mosque and Jawab.

3. The Charbagh garden and surrounding pavilions.

4. A set of tombs.

5. The Taj Ganji

Today, modern visitors enter the monument near the southern gates, starting at the chaotic bazaar before passing through the outer courtyard and through the Great Gate. It is at this point that visitors enter the charbagh garden and view the mausoleum for the first time. Continuing north through the symmetrical gardens, visitors enter the mausoleum before passing through the other side to the Yamuna river and finally across it to the ruins of the moonlight garden.

Taj Ganji (bazaar and caravanserai)

The Taj Mahal is surrounded by an outer perimeter wall made of red sandstone, similar to those at Shah Jahan's other great construction, the nearby Red Fort in Delhi. However, here the walls are more of a symbolic marking off of the territory and not for defense, as they only surround the complex on three sides and are open to the river.[24] Beyond these walls to the east and west is an open, semi-rural area stretching all the way to the Agra Fort. This area has been protected as the "Taj Protected Forest" in order to maintain the historic landscape around these

---

24 "Taj Mahal Perimeter Wall, Taj Mahal, Agra, India," accessed online at:
http://www.flickr.com/photos/davydubbit/4156129564/

two world heritage sites.

There are numerous gates to enter the complex, all dramatic and in a style similar to the famous main gate of the Mausoleum. Called an "iwan", it involves a large ceremonial, decorated arch with a smaller door inside it. The Taj Ganji area within the gates is a bustling bazaar area that was designed in the earliest plans to service the needs of the planned visitors with a market and caravanserai (the equivalent of today's hotels). Throughout the Muslim world, these types of institutions are often constructed alongside a mosque or shrine-tomb, and the money made there is at least partly used for the maintenance of the facility. The resulting closeness between bazaar and charitable institution in the Persian world was seen in modern times in the merchant-priest alliance that was a central core of the Iranian Islamic Revolution of 1979[25]. Today, this area - which is sometimes called Mumtazabad - remains a marketplace teeming with life[26], and it's popular for its budget accommodations and backpacker clientele (tour groups enter from side gates).

The Forecourt (Jilaukhana)

Next, visitors pass through another, grander set of gates and enter a more formal area, today known as the Forecourt or Jilaukhana. This area was designed to be the home of attendants who worked in the Taj facility - a step above the bazaaris of the Taj Ganji but economically tied to them. The buildings and grounds of the tomb and surrounding facilities needed (and still need) constant maintenance, but today, the city of Agra has grown to come right up to the southern gates of the Taj and modern transport means that a class of in-house servants was no longer needed.

There is a small bazaar here, with two colonnaded streets that, until recently, held shops that supported the complex. Additionally, this area has two lesser tombs which appear like miniature versions of the main mausoleums and are said to hold two of Shah Jahan's less favored wives.

On the far side of the Jilaukhana from the Taj Ganji is the entrance to the formal gardens. Called the "Great Gate," ("Darwaza-i rauza") it is an iwan constructed of red sandstone with white marble highlights, a fusion of the style of the red outer walls and echoes of what is to come. By this point, visitors can notice the rectilinear style found throughout the complex: the building has a square footprint and has four identical corner towers. Each of these is topped with a chhatri - a domed pavilion standing on pillars - an element common throughout Mughal architecture and drawn from indigenous Hindu traditions.

---

25 "Bazaaris' Interests in the Iranian Economy: Coalition with the Ulama" by Mehmet Ufuk Tutan (2008). In *Ege Akademik Bakış / Ege Academic Review* (8) 1: 257-266

26 Pictures of Mumtazabad can be seen here: http://taj-mahal.net/augEng/textMM/forecourtengN.htm

Pictures of the Great Gate

This building was designed to mark a transition between two worlds: the outer and the inner, the profane and the sacred, of the living and of the dead. This division and transition are important elements of Islamic spatial and architectural thinking. The outer world is dedicated to commerce and is the space of men, and in this case it consists of the bazaar, while the inner world is one of beauty, gardens and women, which for the Taj consists of the Mausoleum and gardens.

While many Western observers might immediately associate this outside-inside divide with the practice of purdah - the veiling of women from immodest gaze - it is broader than simply that practice. For instance, in the earlier 15th century Topkapı Palace in Istanbul, the home of the Ottoman Sultan, foreign dignitaries passed through various outer courts, moving inwards through gates into deeper levels of privacy, beauty and sanctity until their meeting with the sultan, who was hidden behind a screen. On a much more common level, neighborhoods throughout Islamic cities were often semi-private areas with gates (formal or informal) controlled by the residents; so visitors to the Taj would have been familiar with the concept of moving inwards from the hustle and bustle of the bazaar to the more private realm[27].

The Formal Gardens (Charbagh)

Through the Great Gate, visitors enter one of the most spectacular landscapes on earth: the Gardens of the Taj Mahal. Unlike many famous monuments, such as the Eiffel Tower or the Pyramids of Giza, the Taj Mahal is largely hidden from view and does not dominate the city's landscape. Instead, it is withdrawn inside the walls like a precious gem and is only finally revealed to visitors once they pass through the Great Gate.

Observers stand on a raised stone platform that continues along the perimeter wall, giving a sense that the garden is sunken and giving further drama to the mausoleum rising up in the distance. The garden itself is square, with four paths and pools of water coming in from each of the gates. Also in front of the gate is a long reflecting pool which continually draws the eyes towards the mausoleum. In the very center of the garden, the spot where traditionally one would find the tomb in earlier Mughal garden tombs, is a central fountain. The gardens themselves are perfectly manicured and symmetrical, with lines of shrubbery and trees flanking the approach to the Mausoleum.

---

27 "The Islamic City - Historic Myth, Islamic Essence and Contemporary Relevance" by Janet L. Abu-Lughod (1987) in the *International Journal of Middle East Studies* 19:155-176.

From the courtyards of the Alhambra in Grenada, Spain to the palace of Taman Sari in Indonesia, wherever Muslims have spread, they have constructed beautiful courtyard gardens centered around the display of water, with pools, fountains, basins and streams. The Taj is no exception, and though they will always play second fiddle to the mausoleum, the formal gardens of the Taj Mahal are a beautiful example of a Mughal water garden.

The garden's style is known as a "Charbagh," which means a garden in "fours", as the Charbagh is always divided into four equal quadrants, typically by two streams that meet (or originate) in the center. These are meant to represent the four rivers leading into heaven, because the Qur'an describes the afterlife as akin to being in a garden where there are "rivers of water unstalling" and the deceased "recline upon couches" in gardens, pastures and pavilions. The first Mughal emperor Babur took these metaphors to heart and created a garden tomb which all of his successors copied. The Taj incorporated this tradition, except that it moves the tomb out of its traditional place at the center of the garden and makes the garden a type of forecourt to the tomb itself[28].

Within the context of India, formal gardens have long been associated with royal rule. "Each

---

28 *The Poetics of Gardens* by Charles W. Moore, William J. Mitchell, and William Turnbull   Pp. 179-190

royal garden was a metaphor for the formal symmetry of imperial rule imposed over the turbulent, multi-layered, social landscape of India. Just as the physical landscape was disciplined by the Emperor, so was society."[29] Beyond the Taj Mahal, Shah Jahan was said to have directed the construction of 999 pleasure gardens and it was in his reign that the Mughal Garden tradition reached its apex. All of these gardens were characterized by the traditional Islamic fascination with running water,[30] and even today a number of these and earlier works survive, such as Ram Bagh in Agra, Pinjore Gardens in Haryana, Shalamar Gardens in Lahore and Shalimar Bagh in Srinagar.

Shalamar Gardens, which was constructed on the orders of Shah Jahan between 1641-2, shows a number of similarities to the Taj gardens. It is a walled complex, has a rectilinear overall design, extensively uses flowing waters, and is constructed in a distinct series of terraces aligned south to north, much as the Taj is divided into sections[31]. However, unlike these gardens, the Taj could not be built at the base of a steep incline and thus tap into the natural power of water descending slopes in order to power its fountains and pools. Instead, the Taj uses an elaborate system of ingenious waterworks to achieve the same results[32].

Finally, visitors pass along the reflecting pool up the steps of another raised marble platform to the mausoleum itself. Behind the mausoleum, the land drops away toward the Yamuna River and more gardens, so it appears that there is nothing behind the Taj, which seems to stand alone on the horizon. Since the Taj is a perfectly symmetrical square (with one exception that is discussed below), visitors could approach from any direction, but it is made obvious by the gardens that the designers intended visitors to appreciate it from here.

The imposing facade is dominated by two elements: the soaring iwan gate and, above it, the white marble onion dome. Flanking the dome are two chhatris, below which are decorative balconies. Finally, at the outer edge of the four corners of the platform are the minaret-like spires. The entire structure is constructed in luminous white marble, though from this distance you can already make out hints of the elaborate decorative motifs that adorn the building.

The Main Complex

Of course, when people think about the Taj Mahal, the image immediately brought to mind is the main complex itself, a central area that contains three buildings: the Mausoleum, the Mosque (which is to the left when looking at the complex from the gardens) and the Guesthouse. The Mosque and Guesthouse are, from their exterior, identical structures that maintain the

---

29 *Power, Administration and Finance in Mughal India* by John Richards (1993). Aldershot, England: Vaiorum. Pp 261. Quoted in *In the Time of Trees and Sorrows: Nature, Power and Memory in Rajasthan* by Ann Grodzins Gold and Bhoju Ram Gujar (2002). Duke University Press: Durham and London. Pp 247
30 "Mughal Gardens of Kashmir" accessed online at: http://kashmirimages.net/mughal-gardens-kashmir.html
31 "Fort and Shalamar Gardens in Lahore" on the webpage of the UNESCO World Heritage Site Network. Accessed online at: http://whc.unesco.org/en/list/171/
32 "Taj Mahal Water Devices and Layout," accessed online at: http://www.liveindia.com/tajmahal/water.html

harmonious symmetry of the complex, though the Mosque's interior is different because it faces Mecca.

The interior of the mosque. Picture by Bjørn Christian Tørrissen

After taking photos, the visitor may approach the Mausoleum, but photos are no longer permitted inside the structure itself. The building sits on its own marble plinth, and upon entering through the front gate of the iwan, visitors pass into a small entry room, and from there into a short hallway that enters into the central room of the complex, directly underneath the soaring dome. Within this room is a central area separated from the visitor by a marble screen, and within this screen are the cenotaphs of Mumtaz Mahal and Shah Jahan. The cenotaph of Mumtaz is in the very center of the chamber, while that of the Shah is next to it, slightly offset from center and thus the only non-symmetrical element in the entire structure. These are called "cenotaphs" and not "tombs" because the actual bodies of the two individuals are not located within them but are instead buried in subterranean chambers directly below the visitors' feet. The Mausoleum has a second floor which opens up into exterior balconies and subterranean levels, where the remains of the two are buried, but both of these levels are closed to visitors.

The jali screen in front of the cenotaphs

The cenotaphs

The actual tombs in the subterranean chamber. Picture by William Donelson

The interiors show their great debt to Muslim and Persian art through their elaborate use of decorative tiles and mosaics. In fact, the entire interior is completely covered in elaborate geometric and floral patterns, many of them in stunning colors that contrast with the relative simplicity of the white marble exterior. In addition to these patterns, Muslim artists have always considered calligraphy to be one of their greatest art forms, and it was used extensively in the structure. This is because the traditional Sunni interpretation of the Qur'an has forbidden the depiction of humans or animals to prevent them becoming the objects of worship. This, along with their deep veneration for the Qur'an as the word of God, has meant that they have turned their artistic energies to the depiction of beauty through words themselves. This love of the written word has long been fused with Muslim architecture as well, and the Taj has a number of beautiful pieces of calligraphic inscription drawn entirely from the Qur'an.[33]

---

33 "Taj Mahal Calligraphy" at www.tajmahal.org.uk, accessed online at:
http://www.tajmahal.org.uk/calligraphy.html

A plant motif within the Taj

Decorations adorning the jali screen

Calligraphy inscribed above an arch inside the Taj

Another part of the building that naturally stands out is the dome itself, an important element of Persian architecture (though not widely used in pre-Islamic India)[34]. The greatest surviving dome from Ancient Europe is the one above the Pantheon in Rome, which has a diameter of 142 feet (both around and from floor to ceiling) and was completed in 123 A.D.[35]. Somewhat smaller is the dome of the Hagia Sophia Church/Mosque in Byzantium/Istanbul, with a diameter of 102 feet and completed in 537 AD[36]. The Taj dome is a bit different than these because it is in an "onion" style, which is shared between Persian, Mughal and Eastern Orthodox architecture, and unlike the domes of the Hagia Sophia and the Pantheon, it is not a perfect circle but instead reaches to a point. In total, it reaches up to 144 feet, slightly exceeding that of the Pantheon. However, like Christopher Wren's dome in St. Paul's Cathedral, the Taj's interior actually has a false domed ceiling roughly halfway up the interior. This is meant to maintain a sense of human scale in the interior and allow for decorations to be visible from the floor, all while still maintaining the grand exterior scale of the structure[37].

---

34 "Dome in Iranian Architecture" by Bernard O'Kane. At *the Circle of Ancient Iranian Studies* website. Accessed online at: http://www.cais-soas.com/CAIS/Architecture/dome.htm
35 "Wonders of the World Databank: Dome of the Pantheon" accessed online at: http://www.pbs.org/wgbh/buildingbig/wonder/structure/pantheon.html
36 "Wonders of the World Databank: Dome of the Pantheon" accessed online at: http://www.pbs.org/wgbh/buildingbig/wonder/structure/hagia_sophia.html

The top of the Taj Mahal's dome

The Yamuna River and the Moonlight Garden

Behind the Taj Mahal flows the next element of the site's design: the Yamuna River. While not as famous as the Ganges, the Yamuna (also called the Jumna) River is one of Hinduism's sacred waterways and was an important artery for the traffic of the Mughal Empire, because it flows down from the Himalayas and passes Delhi. Then, as now, the city was the capital - in fact, it had been extensively rebuilt by Shah Jahan - and the proximity of this city was undoubtedly important for the symbolism of the Taj[38]. The Yamuna continued to flow southeast from the capital, flowing past Agra and then winding its way until finally joining the mighty Ganges near Allahabad[39].

---

37 "The Dome of the Mausoleum" accessed online at: http://www.taj-mahal.net/augEng/textMM/domeexteriorengN.htm
38 *Shajahanabad: The Sovereign City in Mughal India 1639-1739* by Stephen P. Blake (2002). Cambridge University Press.
39 "Yamuna River" in the *Encyclopedia Britannica*, accessed online at: http://www.britannica.com/EBchecked/topic/651644/Yamuna-River

Modern observers often compare the rivers of the pre-modern world to highways, but this unfortunately falls short. Today's highways carry travelers and goods efficiently from place to place, which was certainly one of the roles of the rivers, but rivers were also the carriers of information and control in the pre-modern state, as well as providing fish, a place for washing people and clothes, water for cooking, irrigation and drinking, and - in the Hindu tradition - the space for sacred ceremonies, especially cremations and the disposal of the ashes of the deceased. Thus, rivers were absolutely central to life in the Mughal Empire, and undoubtedly Shah Jahan intended to have his great mausoleum viewed as much from the river as from the gardens.

Looking south toward the Taj Mahal with the Yamuna River in the foreground

Of course, since the Mausoleum is perfectly symmetrical, the view from the River is identical to that of the garden. In some ways, it may be even more striking, because those approaching from the river arrive at a lower height than the visitors on foot. The Taj appears to loom over the Yamuna, as its marble terrace is built close to the riverfront and there is no perimeter wall to shield its bulk. Moreover, as there is nothing else on the bank for some distance, it is not crowded by other structures. As the primary artery of the empire, connecting the capital to far-flung territories, it would have been an impressive picture of imperial power for those traveling up to the capital, especially foreign dignitaries who arrived by sea to today's Calcutta and Bengal and then traveled up the Ganges.

On the far side of the Yamuna is the last element of the design: the oft-forgotten Moonlight Gardens. Today there is little here, and in sharp contrast to the immaculate maintenance of the Charbagh, these gardens have fallen into disuse and decay. There is a remnant of a perimeter wall and a single tower surviving here, but aerial imaging has shown that there was once a charbagh here as well that matched the one across the river in size. The central element of the design here was an octagonal pool on the shore directly across from the Mausoleum in which the building's reflection would appear on moonlit nights[40]. Relatively few visitors come here today, since most transportation is not by the river but instead on land, and there are no convenient bridges for visitors at the main area of the Taj's complex.

Chapter 4: The Taj Mahal in Modern Times

After its creation, the Taj Mahal functioned within the Mughal Empire much as it had been intended: a symbol of imperial power along the Yumana River maintained by donations from the government and income from the attached bazaar and caravansary. While it was seen as having historic relevance, it was not seen through the eyes of nostalgia as belonging to a past time, in the same way that the monuments of Washington D.C. are seen as historically valuable by Americans today but are also considered part of the everyday modern symbolic life of the nation, not representing a deceased people, regime or belief system. For the Taj Mahal, however, this began to change as the Mughal government crumbled and other states began to rise up in India to replace it, particularly the British Raj.

In fact, the Taj gained its first protection as a site with a valuable history during the British colonial period, thanks to a group led by famed British Orientalist Sir William Jones, who established the Asiatic Society in 1784 in Calcutta, at that time the capital of British India. During this period, the Mughal Empire had crumbled down to a rump state based around Delhi, and Agra itself was administered by the powerful Maratha state based out of today's Maharastra. By the early 19th century, British power had been expanded to include Agra, Delhi and the Yamuna Valley, and soon after those conquests, the Society appointed Francis Buchanan to survey the monuments of the new territories, including the Taj. The British administration even gave monies to maintain the Taj, one of the very few monuments they financed, perhaps because during this time, it became increasingly popular with British visitors who began to see it as a symbol of romantic love. The famous British writer Rudyard Kipling, a champion of imperialism who wrote at length about British India, described it as "the embodiment of all things pure."

---

40 "The Moonlight Garden: New Discoveries at the Taj Mahal" a review, accessed online at: http://www.the-south-asian.com/Moonlight%20garden.htm

Sir William Jones

The Society worked throughout the 19th century to catalog and analyze the subcontinent's antiquities, and during this time the Taj Mahal became famous throughout first the English-speaking world and then the rest of European and European-influenced societies. By the time of the 1857 Indian Revolt (sometimes called the "Sepoy Rebellion"), the Society had become the "Royal Asiatic Society" and had gained considerable respect in British academic circles. In 1861, when the British Crown had taken over the Indian colonies from the East India Company, they created the first position of Archaeological Surveyor and the Archaeological Survey of India, which was given the power "to prevent injury to and preserve buildings remarkable for their antiquity or for their historical or architectural value."

After Indian Independence, the new Republic kept in place the Archaeological Survey of India (ASI), which became the legal guardian of the Taj Mahal and many other sites. Important protections were set up in the Ancient Monuments and Archaeological Sites and Remains Act of 1958 (with major amendments in 2010) and the Antiquities and Art Treasures Act of 1972[41]. The ASI keeps the site open daily year-round, though on Fridays it is only open to Muslim worshipers at the on-site mosque.[42]

Today, the Taj is primarily experienced as a tourist attraction, and it brings in over 2 million domestic and over 400,000 foreign visitors a year. It is the most popular single attraction in the country, closely followed by two nearby Mughal sites: the Agra Fort and the Red Fort[43]. Studies

---

41 "History" at the Homepage of the Archaeological Survey of India. Accessed online at: http://asi.nic.in/asi_aboutus_history.asp
42 "World Heritage Sites - Agra - Taj Mahal" at the *Archaeological Survey of India* accessed online at: http://asi.nic.in/asi_monu_whs_agratajmahal.asp

of these visitors show that not only are they diverse in their national origin, but also in the ways that they interpret the importance and meaning of the site. While it is true that most interpret the site along the popular "symbol of love" narrative, others see it as a symbol of Muslim power and still others as an emblem of a lost colonial era.[44] These symbolic perspectives also take on new flavors as they are continually adopted and twisted about in new circumstances. For example, in 1992, Princess Diana visited the Taj and had a number of solitary photos taken of her on a bench. As her marriage to Prince Charles was disintegrating in a very public way at the time, her solitude in the world's preeminent symbol of royal loneliness and lost love became instantly famous[45].

At the same time, the Taj also remains a pre-eminent symbol of India, as evidenced by the innumerable Indian restaurants around the globe named for it (perhaps rivaled only by the number of Chinese restaurants named for the Great Wall), its appearances on packages of frozen Indian food, not to mention endless amounts of tourist kitsch. In contrast to these commercialized uses of the site, the ASI has done its best to fight commercialization, specifically because of the site's importance as a national symbol not to be appropriated by brands. As a result, the ASI forbids all sorts of promotional uses and forbids product placement and advertising photo shoots at the site. In 2013, the ASI even lodged a police complaint against the reigning Miss Universe, Olivia Culpo, when she smuggled shoes she was advertising into the site and had photos taken of her in them in front of the building[46].

Despite its close association with India, or perhaps because of it, the fact that what is easily India's most famous structure was built by a Muslim dynasty and not an indigenous Hindu one rankles the Hindu far-right. This conservative movement, called "Hindutva," has sought to denigrate, minimize or outright erase the presence of Muslims in Northern India, both in the present day and also in the historic and architectural record. The most shocking example of this was when an anti-Muslim mob literally tore apart the Mughal Babri Mosque in Ayodhya, claiming that it was built on the site of an earlier Hindu temple to the god Ram. This led to religious strife and riots throughout India that resulted in the deaths of hundreds.

A similar claim was forcefully made by amateur historian P.N. Oak throughout much of the 20th century about the Taj Mahal. He argued that the building was literally a Hindu palace-

---

43 "Romantic Taj Mahal attracts maximum visitors in India" at theindian.com (2008). Accessed online at: http://www.thaindian.com/newsportal/world-news/romantic-taj-mahal-attracts-maximum-visitors-in-india_10075652.html
44 *Tourists at the Taj: Performance and Meaning at a Symbolic Site* by Tim Edensor. Routledge. London, New York.
45 The images of Lady Di at the Taj can be seen here: http://iconicphotos.wordpress.com/2009/05/25/diana-at-the-taj-mahal/
46 "Pictured: The Moment American Miss Universe took part in 'disrespectful' high heels photo shoot in protected grounds of the Taj Mahal" by James Nye. 8 October 2013 in the *Daily Mail* accessed online at: http://www.dailymail.co.uk/news/article-2450447/Pictured-Miss-Universes-disrespectful-Taj-Mahal-photo-shoot.html

temple that was converted by Shah Jahan into a tomb, and that an anti-Hindu conspiracy prevented him from opening sealed tombs and revealing that they were full of Hindu relics. He went even further by arguing that every single Muslim building in India was in fact a Hindu building that had been converted to Muslim use, while also asserting that both Islam and Christianity were perverted forms of Hinduism and that both the Vatican and Westminster Abbey were also Hindu temples[47]. While Oak's writing has no basis in architectural or archival history, it has been taken up by members of the same anti-Muslim movement and continues to resurface regularly since his death in 2007, with modern claims that Shah Jahan was actually a closet Hindu[48]. In recent years, a North American Hindu convert named Stephen Knapp has taken up the issue of the Taj as a "Vedic temple," making his argument by cherry-picking images of the Taj's decorations, emphasizing the Hindu elements of the architecture, and completely ignoring the building's style, history and overall decor[49]. It must be emphasized by any calm examiner of the building that these theories hold no water and are malicious attempts to undermine the already vulnerable position of India's Muslims and legitimize both the destruction of their heritage and physical attacks against them.

Of course, not all modern manipulations of the Taj have been so troubling. The site has even been host to occasional bouts of playfulness. In 2000, PC Sorcar Jr., an Indian stage magician, created an illusion during which the Taj disappeared from view, delighting visitors. [50]

Alongside these debates and symbolic uses, the world status of the Taj Mahal has only been strengthened and confirmed in recent years. In 1983, the United Nations Educational, Scientific and Cultural Organization (UNESCO) recognized the Taj Mahal as part of its list of World Heritage Sites, stating that it represents "a masterpiece of human creative genius." While the list was created in 1972, India only began submitting sites to it in 1983, so it was amongst the first crop of Indian listees (alongside the nearby Agra Fort, the Ellora Caves and the Ajanta Caves).[51] A less august honor was the opening of the Trump Taj Mahal casino in Atlantic City New Jersey in 1990[52], the Taj Mahal Palace and Tower in Mumbai in 1903, and the Taj Mahal Hotel in Delhi[53] ; all of these institutions tap into the idea of the Taj as the representation of Indian/Oriental royal splendor and luxury.

Recognition has continued into the new millennium. In 2007, the Taj was named as one of the "New7Wonders," a list that was created through a global campaign of online voting. Over 100

---

47 "Taj Mahal - The True Story" at the P.N. Oak homepage. Accessed online at: http://www.pnoak.com/
48 Two examples include: http://defence.pk/threads/did-vaastu-influence-the-building-of-the-taj.6420/ and http://news.bbc.co.uk/dna/place-lancashire/plain/A5220
49 Mr. Knapp's website can be found here: http://www.stephen-knapp.com/
50 "Taj Mahal Disappears Under Magic Spell" at the BBC News Homepage. 10 November 2000. Accessed online at: http://news.bbc.co.uk/2/hi/world/monitoring/media_reports/1017250.stm
51 "Taj Mahal" on the webpage of the UNESCO World Heritage Site Network. Accessed online at: http://whc.unesco.org/en/list/252
52 Homepage at: http://www.trumptaj.com/
53 Hompeage at: http://www.tajhotels.com/

million votes were cast, and the modern list included Chichén Itzá, the Christ the Redeemer statue in Rio de Janeiro, the Great Wall of China, Machu Picchu, the Colosseum, and the ruins of Petra in Jordan[54]. The campaign galvanized international interest and demonstrates how the Taj is able to command loyalty from numerous visitors and fans.

Because it stands so central to the world's imagination of India, those who have sought to attack India have, at times, threatened the Taj. During World War II, the British covered the dome with a protective scaffolding, but the feared Japanese invasion of India was turned back in Assam. In 1971, there was fear about the role of the building in war. India was supporting the partition of Pakistan and Bangladesh, and it was feared that Pakistani planes flying over northern India would use the building as a navigational landmark - especially because it is so luminescent at night. In response, the structure was shrouded in black[55]. In 2001, plans were put into motion to repeat this "camouflage" in case of another war[56]. That said, there was never a fear that the Pakistanis would destroy the building, since it represents a triumphal example of their own Muslim ancestors' architectural and political apogee.

Scaffolding over the Taj Mahal to protect it during wartime

---

54 "New Seven Wonders of the World announced" in *The Telegraph* accessed online at: http://www.telegraph.co.uk/travel/artsandculture/737699/New-Seven-Wonders-of-the-World-announced.html
55 "The Taj Mahal during wars" by younews.in Accessed online at: http://www.tajmahal.gov.in/architecture2.html
56 "Taj Mahal 'to be camouflaged'" at the BBC News Homepage. 29 December 2001. Accessed online at: http://news.bbc.co.uk/2/hi/south_asia/1732993.stm

The first real threat to the building came in 1984, when Punjabi Sikhs seeking to create their own Sikh-controlled state were besieged in the Harmandir Sahib (the "Golden Temple") in the city of Amritsar. The government stormed the building, creating outrage amongst Sikhs around the globe. While the operation was successful in putting down the open revolt, it created widespread anti-government sentiments amongst Sikhs and led to a number of Sikh nationalist groups. One result was the assassination of the Prime Minister Indira Gandhi by her Sikh bodyguards, and in this context, it was feared that the Taj, the ultimate symbol of Indian power and splendor, would be attacked out of revenge for damage done to the Harmandir Sahib[57].

More recently, the site has also been targeted by militant Sunni Muslims claiming affinity to Al-Qaeda. These groups see the Persian and Shiite-inspired shrine as a glorification of a mortal and therefore a distraction from true Islam; the fact that it has become a symbol of India, the rival of (overwhelmingly Sunni) Muslim Pakistan, only makes it a better target.[58] These threats became more tangible after the Taliban's destruction of the Buddhas of Bamiyan in 2001, which showed that the fundamentalists were not afraid of world censure in destroying what they saw as heretical monuments. More distant in time, but still fresh in the minds of Shiite Muslims, was the destruction of a holy cemetery in Mecca by like-minded Saudi Wahhabi fundamentalists in 1925. They declared that despite the fact that the Prophet Mohammed's family was buried at the site, veneration there was not explicitly mentioned in the Qur'an and was therefore heretical. In 2013, the ASI banned foreign visitors to Friday prayers in the mosque.[59]

The reality of Sunni fundamentalist threat to India was most prominently on display in 2008, when a militant group struck the Taj Mahal Palace Hotel, burning the building and killing over 30 people. The fact that the building had been named for the Taj and echoed it architecturally in its dome and chhatri corner towers highlighted the fact that it was a symbolic attack against an image of India.[60]

On a daily basis, however, the greatest threats to the Taj are an increasing number of preservation issues. While the building appears indomitable, there are a number of reasons why its stability is threatened. In 2011, it was reported that because of the fact that the Yamuna River was increasingly running dry due to drought, deforestation and water diversion, the mahogany foundation supports were drying out and weakening. In response, cracks were beginning to appear on the building's surface, and the minarets were beginning to tilt on their foundations. The government has established a campaign of reforestation, but the final results are not in yet.[61]

---

57 Reuters. 16 July 1991. "Police Fear Terrorist Threat to India's Taj Mahal." (NEXIS)
58 "Al-Qaeda Threatens to Blow up Taj Mahal: Indian Parliament also on hit list" 21 December 2007. Accessed online at: http://english.ohmynews.com/articleview/article_view.asp?no=381273&rel_no=1
59 "ASI bans foreigners from Friday namaz at Taj Mahal" by Faisal Fareed at *The Indian Express*. Accessed online: http://www.indianexpress.com/news/asi-bans-foreigners-from-friday-namaz-at-taj-mahal/1212654/
60 "Timeline: Mumbai Under Attack" BBC News Online. 1 December 2008. Accessed online at: http://news.bbc.co.uk/2/hi/south_asia/7754438.stm
61 "Taj Mahal could collapse within five years because wooden foundations are rotting" by James Tapper in *The Daily Mail* 5 October 2011. Accessed online at: http://www.dailymail.co.uk/news/article-2045183/Taj-Mahal-

Another threat comes in the form of acid rain, specifically due to pollutants created by an oil refinery in Mathura. The acidic quality of the rain erodes the relatively soft marble rock and damages the building's carvings.[62] In 1996, the building was added to the World Monument Fund's "Watch List" due to these problems and chronic mismanagement, but since that time the Fund has reported steady progress in documenting the site and organizing its management.[63]

Bibliography

Asher, Catherine B. Architecture of Mughal India New Cambridge History of India I.4, Cambridge University Press 1992

Carroll, David (1971). The Taj Mahal, Newsweek Books

Gascoigne, Bamber (1971). The Great Moguls, Harper & Row.

Koch, Ebba (2006) [Aug 2006]. The Complete Taj Mahal: And the Riverfront Gardens of Agra (First ed.). Thames & Hudson Ltd.,

Lall, John (1992). Taj Mahal, Tiger International Press.

Preston, Diana & Michael (2007) A Teardrop on the Cheek of Time (First ed.). London: Doubleday

Rothfarb, Ed (1998). In the Land of the Taj Mahal, Henry Holt

Tillitson, G.H.R. (1990). Architectural Guide to Mughal India, Chronicle Books.

---

collapse-5-years-wooden-foundations-rotting.html?ITO=1490
62 "Environmental Impact on Taj Mahal stalls Indian Oil's Mathura Refinery Expansion" 30 September 2008. Accessed online at: http://www.industrialinfo.com/news/abstract.jsp?newsitemID=139464
63 "Taj Mahal" at the World Monuments Fund Website. Accessed online at: http://www.wmf.org/project/taj-mahal